Shake, Ripple & Roll

A Rock & Roll Musical

Book and Lyrics by Jenifer Toksvig
Music by David Perkins

Samuel French — London
New York - Toronto - Hollywood

ISBN 0 573 08112 3

SHAKE, RIPPLE & ROLL

First performed at the Yvonne Arnaud Theatre, Guildford on
24th June 1999 by the Yvonne Arnaud Youth Theatre ACT 2,
with the following cast:

Principals (in order of appearance)

Dirk Manley	Matthew Veira
Joey Nobody	Philip Bishop
Mr Cohen	Sarah Dodson
Cherry	Alice Cook
Peaches	Laura Seymour
Pumpkin	Natalie Bolding
Honey	Jenny May
Chuck	Kit Stokes
Deanna la Domme	Holly Rubenstein
Max The Chauffeur	Max Southworth
Doo-Doo The Dog	Herself
Deanna's Boys	Harry Burgess, Jonathan Slater

Chorus (in alphabetical order)

Aurora Denver	Lizzie Bourne
Ida Hoe	Jo Brady
Virginia State	Amanda Duffield
Louisie Anna	Maddie Fenner
Sandy Ago	Lucy Hill
Dee Troit	Marie Kenyan
Minnie Sota	Vicki Lazzari
Della Ware	Emma Lumb
India Nappolis	India McClellan
Harry Zona	Robert O'Donovan
Cally Fornia	Olivia Oldroyd
Holly Wood	Tara Scholes
Atlanta Georgia	Adele Sinclair
Ken Tucky	Robert Slater
Sweet Georgia	Sarah Slater
Beverley Hills	Katy Thorncroft
Minnie Appolis	Hannah Turner
Carol Liner	Lucy Willis
Missy Sippy	Jo Wright

(The Yvonne Arnaud Youth Theatre ACT 2 comprises local
children aged between 7 and 14)

Directed by Julia Burgess
Assistant Director Jenifer Toksvig
Musical Director David Perkins
Lighting Design by John Harris
Sound Design by Dan Last

IMPORTANT INFORMATION

Alterations to the script or score
If changes, additions or cuts to the show are required to make it work for a particular group, any proposed alterations MUST be approved by the authors before rehearsals commence. Approval can be sought via Samuel French Ltd (Musical Plays Department) or directly from the authors via email. An email link for Jenifer Toksvig and David Perkins can be found at their website:www.toksvig-perkins.com

The authors are happy to provide suggestions for such things as song cuts, scene change music, additional character names and so on. Making contact with them is easy, and they will consider any request. Making small changes this way is free of charge and it turns an illegal alteration into a legal one.

Cover illustration
Please note that the cover illustration remains the copyright of the artist, Simon Pearsall, who may be contacted through Samuel French Ltd or via the authors' website at www.toksvig-perkins.com His permission MUST be obtained prior to use of this illustration for publicity purposes, programmes, website graphics, or any other purpose whatsoever.

Director's Credit
The original director, Julia Burgess, compiled the Director's Notes for this libretto. It is a condition of the performing licence that the following credit be used on all programmes and posters for *Shake, Ripple & Roll*:

Originally directed and choreographed by Julia Burgess

Costume Hire
Costumes from the original production at the Yvonne Arnaud Theatre, Millbrook, Guildford, Surrey, GU1 3UX, are available for hire. Please contact the theatre direct.

Video and Audio Recording
In certain circumstances permission may be given for a video or audio recording of your show to be made. Please apply to Samuel French Ltd for full details. Video and audio recordings made without prior permission are STRICTLY not allowed, even for archival or training purposes.

Toksvig-Perkins Musicals

The authors' website at www.toksvig-perkins.com has photographs of the original production, sound bites and other useful information (including details of other shows written by Toksvig-Perkins). Jenifer and David welcome your comments in their message board and guestbook, as well as emailed photographs of *your* production.

Other musicals by Jenifer Toksvig and David Perkins, published by
Samuel French Ltd:

The Curious Quest for the Sandman's Sand
Skool & Crossbones
Pandemonium! *(a Greek Myth-Adventure)*

DIRECTOR'S NOTES

CHARACTER BREAKDOWN

The show can be adapted to suit the number of children you wish to have in the cast. The chorus roles can be played by one group or split into different groups, thus allowing more children to take part. Although all parts should be played by children, some of the characters are "adults" and should be portrayed accordingly.

All characters should speak in an American accent (Standard American/New York area).

MAIN PARTS (in order of appearance)
Dirk Manley ("adult" character)
Typical, black and white movie, private investigator of the 1940s: cool, confident, and incompetent! He narrates the story as well as taking part in it, but is always in character. He needs to have a strong rock and roll singing voice, good comic timing, and the ability to communicate with an audience.
SONGS: Undercover Blues (solo)

Joey Nobody ("adult" character)
Joey, the soda jerk, is a keen and helpful character who is the butt of everyone's humour. With no memory of his past, Uncle Angelo's is his home and the staff and customers are his family. Although he's never credited with it, Joey is the one who comes up with all the solutions to their problems. He should have a very strong singing voice and good acting ability, including great comic timing.
SONGS: Another Day (solo); Shake, Ripple & Roll; Angelo's an Angel Now; Where There's a Will; Nobody's Lament (solo); Undercover Blues; Today's the Day; Nobody's Lament (Reprise — solo)

Mr Cohen ("adult" character)
A comedy character, Mr Cohen is the grumpy manager of Uncle Angelo's. Although he seems harsh at times, he has given Joey a job and a home— and therefore has a good heart. Everyone respects him, despite the fact that his idea of managing the store is shouting at Joey and the waitresses, whilst sitting on the same stool every day, reading his newspaper. He needs to have a strong singing voice and good comic facial expressions.

SONGS: Another Day (solo); Shake, Ripple & Roll; Angelo's an Angel Now (solo); Where There's a Will (solo); Undercover Blues; Today's the Day

Cherry, Peaches, Pumpkin and Honey ("teenage" characters)
The four waitresses; these girls speak and act as one. They are cute, giggly and bubble-headed, more inclined to gossip about movie stars and make-up than they are to take orders in the ice-cream parlour. Joey and the customers love them, Chuck flirts with them and they drive Mr Cohen nuts. They should have reasonable singing ability and speak in squeaky voices.
SONGS: Another Day (solo); Will He Find Me (sing along); Shake, Ripple & Roll; Angelo's an Angel Now; Where There's a Will; Undercover Blues; Today's the Day

Chuck ("teenage" character)
The leader of a gang of kids who hang out at the ice-cream parlour, Chuck is Mr Cool. All the girls love him and the boys (especially Joey) wish they could be him. He should have a strong singing voice and good acting ability.
SONGS: Another Day; Shake, Ripple & Roll (solo); Angelo's an Angel Now; Where There's a Will; Undercover Blues; Today's the Day

Deanna la Domme ("adult" character)
She's a star of the screen, a movie queen! A typical 1950s' movie star: rich, snooty and cunning. She expects everyone to fall at her feet and worship her— and when they do, she walks all over them. Her true colours show through the crocodile tears she produces for effect. This should be indicated by two distinct styles of dialogue: one totally over the top — a ham actress — and one nasty, conniving, scheming, greedy lady! She should have a very strong solo singing voice and good acting ability.
SONGS: Where There's a Will (solo); Deanna (solo)

Max ("adult" character)
Deanna's timid chauffeur, he spends the entire show being a "Yes" man— until he finally plucks up enough courage to become a "No" man at the end! He should have good physical comedy skills and the ability to dance (preferably tap dance).
SONGS: Deanna

Deanna's Boys ("adult" characters)
This is a group which can be played by two or more children, as required. It is also possible to cut these characters and replace their role with Max. They are typical movie star bodyguards... stupid, strong and silent. They should have good dancing ability.
SONGS: Deanna (mostly dance, very little singing)

CHORUS ROLES ("teenage" characters)
They are the customers at Uncle Angelo's, and should appear to be a group of typical 1950s' kids. As the scenes of dialogue between the main characters take place, the customers sit around the edge of the set, miming discussion and reacting to the main action. Customer lines of dialogue are scattered throughout the text, and can be given out to chorus members as required.

Groups of Chorus
Ideally, the chorus should consist of one large group, from which Deanna's Boys and the *Somethin' Strange is Goin' On* singers are taken. The customers should be the same faces each day, to emphasize that they regularly frequent Uncle Angelo's. However, the customers can be split into separate groups if necessary, to give more children the chance to be involved in the production. The show allows for a maximum of six chorus groups (one of which would be Deanna's Boys). Fewer than this is recommended. However, here are suggestions for a maximum of six divisions:

Full Company / Group #1
No.1 **Another Day** can be used to introduce the entire company, or provide an ensemble number for a group of any size and age. All but Group #1 can exit at the end of this number if required.

Group #1
On stage at end of **No.1 Another Day** Page 5
Dialogue
No.2 Shake, Ripple & Roll
Dialogue
No.3 Angelo's an Angel Now
Dialogue
Exit on Page 14

Group #2
Enter on Page 14
Dialogue
No 4 Where There's a Will
Dialogue
Exit on Page19

Group #3
Enter on Page 22
Dialogue
No.6 Undercover Blues
Dialogue
No.7 Somethin' Strange is Goin' On (frozen in the background)
Exit the end of the song Page 29

Group #4 (school choir/strong singers — to join Group #3)
Enter on Page 28 for **Somethin' Strange is Goin' On**
Exit on Page 29 at the end of the song

Group #5
Enter on Page 29
No.8 **Today's The Day** & rest of show

Group #6 — Deanna's Boys (to join Group #5)
Enter on Page 30
Dialogue
No. 9 **Deanna** & rest of show

Full company
Enter on Page 39
Reprise of No. 12 **Shake, Ripple & Roll** and curtain calls

SONG NOTES

No. 1 Another Day
This is a light, upbeat number used to introduce the main characters in their environment as the store opens for business
No. 1a Will He Find Me?
Although they only join in with the jukebox song for three lines of the chorus, it is important that the few words the waitresses sing should be clear and audible.
No. 2 Shake, Ripple & Roll
A typical rock and roll song. The chorus should be encouraged to do some hand-jiving!
No. 3 Angelo's an Angel Now
A spoof gospel choir style song. The chorus should be encouraged to use expressive angelic faces and poses.
No. 4 Where There's a Will
A tango-style number during which Mr Cohen and Deanna should dance together... to the obvious displeasure of Mr Cohen. The dance steps could be symbolic of a struggle between these two main characters. The chorus can repeat simple, staccato tango steps in the background, split into two vocal/dance groups to enhance the sense of conflict. If preferred, they can stand frozen in a tango tableau for this number.
No. 5 Nobody's Lament
This is the moment where the audience should feel great sympathy for Joey. He is alone in the store at night-time, so it should have a sense of intimacy which can be created by lighting only a small area around him. Movement for this number should be minimal, to assist focus on the pathos of the song.

No. 6 Undercover Blues
An uptempo, rock and roll number in true Elvis style which should get the audience clapping along in time to the music! It's a great opportunity to make use of the dancing skills of the chorus. Joey and Mr Cohen, or a group of the chorus, can mime jazz instruments during this number.

No. 7 Somethin' Strange is Goin' On
This is a moment of Suspension of Disbelief: a commentary, set outside the action in Uncle Angelo's. A barbershop song, it can be sung by an entirely separate choir if preferred, and they need not necessarily enter through the main "door". Movement should be minimal, to place the emphasis on vocals. There are two versions of this song: one slightly more complicated than the other in harmony. Either can be used, according to the vocal ability of the chorus group. See vocal score and Composer's Notes for more details.

No. 8 Today's the Day
An up-tempo number to indicate the passage of a few days, and to heighten suspense as the tension mounts. Movement could be slightly jazzy and repetitive to indicate the frustrations of the customers. The instrumental breaks between the verses can be used to create a sense of the passage of time with use of rhythmic and random pacing.

No. 9 Deanna
Hollywood meets Broadway in this Busby Berkeley style vehicle for Deanna la Domme and her boys. This number should be extravagant, glitzy and over the top!

No. 10 The Will
Music enhances the final, desperate attempt to save the store. As they search, their movement can be very stylized, similar to the instrumental breaks of No 8. **Today's the Day**. The audience must have a clear view of both the coat hook and the jukebox as Joey triggers the secret panel which reveals the safe. The final dialogue during this instrumental piece is very specifically set into the music, as per the vocal score.

No. 11 Nobody's Lament (reprise)
Everyone else freezes as Joey has a moment of solitary realization: his dreams have finally come true. The focus should be entirely on Joey as he takes centre stage to share his thoughts with the audience.

PROPERTIES
A list of properties can be found on page 41. Many are essential to the show. However, they can be as simple or elaborate as resources allow, and may provide the opportunity for students to do some research into America in the 1950s.

COSTUME
A suggested costume plot is indicated on page 43. Costumes can be simplified according to the available resources. In their simplest form:

circular skirts for the girls, blue jeans for the boys, aprons for the waitresses and baseball boots and T-shirts for all! Should such be necessary for Deanna's Boys, an opportunity to exit for costume change is marked in the script. Again, costuming this show may provide the opportunity for students to do some research.

LIGHTING AND EFFECTS
No. 1a Will He Find Me?
FX: Will He Find Me? (needle stuck)
This is the only song which the old jukebox plays. A cassette tape, available on hire from Samuel French Ltd, contains the complete track of this song, as well as a special effect of the jukebox needle jumping on a scratch over the title line. *These two taped effects must be used in the production.* The music appears in the vocal score for learning purposes.

An American telephone rings with a repeated single tone, as opposed to the British double tone. This is also included on the sound effect tape —
Telephone Rings (FX)

The sound of an American street, footsteps, cars and horns etc. may be used to create low atmospherics in the background at various points during the show. These points are indicated in the script and the Effects Plot (Page 48). This track can be raised briefly every time the "door" is opened throughout the show, and must be faded out as indicated. When playing, it must be at a very low level so as not to distract from the dialogue and action.

SET
A plan of the original staging can be found on Page 41.

With thanks to Julia Burgess for the preparation of the Director's Notes.

COMPOSER'S NOTES
Metronome markings have been printed in the Piano/Vocal Score to indicate the tempo for each song. In order to recreate the appropriate style and feeling for each song it is strongly recommended that these are adhered to as closely as possible.

The song **No. 7 Something Strange is Going On** appears in the Piano/Vocal Score in two versions. The second version is the simpler of the two and should be used if the singers are musically less experienced or few in number. The first version splits into three parts in bars 19–27. Use this if the singers are more experienced but put more people on the top stave to help to bring out the words in bars 19–22.

Shake, Ripple & Roll has been scored for a four-piece rock and roll band: Piano, Drums, Bass (Electric and/or Acoustic) and Reeds (Alto Sax and Clarinet in Bb). An Electric or Acoustic Guitar could also be added playing from the chord symbols in the Vocal Score. A keyboard could be used to add extra sounds on top of the main piano part. For example, Jazz Organ in numbers 2 and 6, Vibes for the right hand in number 8 and on the "revelation chords" in number 10.

If necessary, the show can be performed with a reduced line-up. For example, Piano, Bass and Drums or Piano and Drums or just Piano alone.

AMERICAN REFERENCE NOTES
GLOSSARY OF TERMS

Schmo	Dogsbody
Oy vey!	A Yiddish exclamation of exasperation
Poodle skirts	Circular felt skirts with a Poodle appliqué made of fluffy wool
Thunderbirds	Ford made this popular car
Saddle shoes	Oxford shoe with a two-colour pattern, rather like golfing shoes
Pretzel	A salty dough snack, often made in a knot or rod shape
Sarsaparilla	A vanilla-flavoured fizzy drink
Dairy Queen	A brand of soft ice-cream
Kelvinator	A brand of refrigerator
Sheesh	A Yiddish exclamation of dismay or frustration
Soda jerk	The man who made the sodas (jerking the pumps)
Mall	A shopping centre
Dues	Debt

Nice and a token will get you on the subway   Implying that "nice" is worthless and when added to a subway token, will still only get you on the subway

ICE-CREAM PARLOUR PRODUCTS
Certain products were very specifically "New York" in the 1950s. These can be written on the menus or used as advertisements on posters etc:

2-cents plain	Plain soda water
Egg Creams	Seltzer water (soda), "U Bet" chocolate syrup and milk
Pretzel rods	2 for a cent
Malteds	Flavoured milkshakes with malt syrup
Hamburgers	25c with everything on it
Hot dogs	25c with everything on it
Cherry coke	Coke with cherry syrup — 10c

Chocolate coke	Coke with chocolate syrup — 10c
Royal Crown cola	A brand name of cola
	(bottles only had "RC" on them)
Pepsi Cola	Advertisements were often
	on a bright yellow background
Nickel cokes	Short bottles of coke for 5c
Sarsaparilla	Vanilla soda — 10c
Popsicles	Ice lollies — 7c
Penny Candy	Various kinds for 1c
Snow Cones	Crushed ice with flavoured syrup
	in cone-shaped paper cups
French Fries	Chips

COINAGE

Penny	1c
Nickel	5c
Dime	10c
Quarter	25c

MUSICAL NUMBERS

No. 1	**Another Day**	Joey, Mr Cohen, Waitresses, Ensemble
No. 1a	Will He Find Me?	Waitresses
No. 2	**Shake, Ripple & Roll**	Chuck, Ensemble
No. 3	**Angelo's an Angel Now**	Mr Cohen, Ensemble
No. 4	**Where There's a Will**	Mr Cohen, Deanna, Ensemble
No. 5	**Nobody's Lament**	Joey
No. 6	**Undercover Blues**	Dirk Manley, Ensemble
No. 7	**Somethin' Strange is Goin' On**	Chorus Group
No. 8	**Today's the Day**	Chorus
No. 9	**Deanna**	Deanna, Max, Deanna's Boys
No. 10	The Will (instrumental underscore)	
No. 11	**Nobody's Lament (reprise)**	Joey
No. 12	**Finale (Reprise: Shake, Ripple & Roll)**	Ensemble
No. 12a	Bows	
No. 12b	**Encore (Reprise: Another Day)**	Ensemble
No. 12c	Exit Music	

The vocal score and band parts are available on hire from Samuel French Ltd.

ACKNOWLEDGEMENTS

Jenifer and David would like to thank the following
people for their continuing support:

Our families and loved ones

The Yvonne Arnaud Theatre, Guildford
James Barber, Director of YAT
The ACT 2 kids (and their parents!)
Seamus "Instant Sets" Benson and the crew

The very creative Simon Pearsall

… and last but most importantly…

Julia Burgess, without whom none of this would have
been half as silly, half as much fun, or half as successful.

For John and Caroline

SHAKE, RIPPLE & ROLL

The interior of a 1950s ice- cream parlour, in a small town just outside New York City (probably on Long Island)

The parlour is a popular meeting place for the local teenage kids when the summer is hot and the shakes are cool. As the only location in the show, the set should contain some levels to provide variation in staging if possible: stairs, rostra, etc. There is one main entrance, UC, through which the customers and staff arrive and leave. There is another exit / entrance which leads to the stockroom. (See original stage plan and Furniture and Property list for more information)

The narrator (Dirk Manley) stands DS separately from the main scene

A pool of light, as if from a streetlamp, comes up on the narrator

Dirk Manley *(narrating)* The name's Manley. Dirk Manley. I'm a Private Investigator, but don't hold that against me. I wanna tell you a little story.

The Lights change to a general morning full-stage wash

This story happened a long, long time ago. I'll never forget that year. It was — err — it was — '56! Yeah, that's right. Summer of '56.

No.1

A sax solo begins to underscore (optional)

Hot, ya know what I'm sayin'? The kids were all on summer vacation, and they used to hang out at this place: Uncle Angelo's ice-cream parlour.

As Dirk begins to talk about the "kid", Joey Nobody enters through the stock room entrance. He carries a red and white striped fast food paper hat. As Joey lives in the store, he should always use this entrance. Oblivious to Dirk, he goes to take an apron from behind the bar and puts it on. Forgetting to put on his hat, he picks up a broom

A kid had just started working there, a funny lookin' kid. He just walked
in off a the street one day, in a kinda daze. Seems he'd bumped his head
on somethin' and lost his memory. Didn't even know his own name. The
manager, Mr Cohen, he took pity on the poor kid, gave him a job and a
name. They called him Joey, Joey Nobody, and every morning he'd be up
real early — cleaning — and sweeping — and dreaming about owning the
store someday...

Joey sweeps as he sings

Another Day

Joey   Another day
Gotta clean and sweep.
Another day
Gotta earn my keep.
Every day, up before the sun
I'll see it set before my day is done.
It's just another day, cleaning up the store,
Another day, no different than before.
I'm just a Joe to Uncle Angelo.
Uh-o uh-o
Don't wanna be a rock and roll star.
Don't wanna drive a Chevrolet car.
Wanna run the show for Uncle Angelo
Uh-o uh-o
They say that I'm a fool, but that ain't so.
One day I'll tell them all where they can go.
Uh-o
A-whoa whoa whoa whoa whoa

*Mr Cohen, the manager, enters. He carries a newspaper which he often
buries himself behind, lowering it only to speak or sing*

The music continues to underscore the following dialogue

Mr Cohen Morning, Joey.
Joey Morning, Mr Cohen, sir!
Dirk Manley (*narrating*) Mr Cohen, the manager, was a nice guy but a little
bit — touchy. Ya know what I mean?
Joey It's gonna be a beautiful day, sir!
Mr Cohen Never mind beautiful day, Joey, did ya clean the pumps yet?
Joey I'm just doing them now, sir!

Mr Cohen Well, get a move on. We'll have a bunch'a kids here any minute!
Joey Yes, sir!

Mr Cohen (*singing*) It's just another day, managing the store,
        Another day, no different than before.
        I'm just a schmo for Uncle Angelo
        Uh-o uh-o
        Summer's here, all the kids in town
        With dimes and nickels come to hang around
        And spend their dough for Uncle Angelo
        Uh-o uh-o
        Joey's just a kid but even so
        He didn't have no other place to go.
        Uh-o
        A-whoa whoa whoa whoa whoa

Cherry, Peaches, Pumpkin and Honey, the waitresses, enter

The music continues to underscore the following dialogue

Cherry Morning ——
Peaches — Morning ——
Pumpkin — Morning ——
Honey — Morning ——
All 4 Girls — Mr Cohen, sir!
Mr Cohen Cherry, Peaches, Pumpkin, Honey. You're late, girls. Ain't
  nobody got a watch?
Joey No, sir, I don't have a watch.

The four waitresses giggle at Joey

Waitresses He didn't mean you, silly.
Mr Cohen Oy vey! What's with the giggling? We open up in three minutes.
  Everybody get to work!
Waitresses ⎫
Joey   ⎬ (*together*)Yes, sir!

The waitresses fetch their notepads and pencils from the bar

Dirk Manley (*narrating*) Cherry, Peaches, Pumpkin and Honey, four of the
  cutest waitresses that I ever saw ——
Joey Good-morning, ladies!
Waitresses Morning, Mr Nobody! (*They giggle*)

Dirk Manley (*narrating*) — but, boy did they tease Joey.

Waitresses (*singing*) It's just another day, serving at the store,
Another day, no different than before.
Ice-cream to go from Uncle Angelo
Uh-o uh-o

We'd adore to date the dreamy guys
Who hang around with lovin' in their eyes.
But who says "No"? Our Uncle Angelo
Uh-o uh-o

We're oh so cute, with rosy cheeks that glow.
We curl our hair like Marilyn Monroe.
Uh-o
A-whoa whoa whoa whoa whoa

The music continues to underscore the following dialogue

Mr Cohen OK, it's time to open up. Joey, go put on your hat. Girls, quit
dancing around, would ya?

Joey fetches his hat

*A crowd of teenage kids enter (plus other assorted customers if required).
This can be the full company or a part of the chorus. First into the store is
Chuck, the leader of a gang of kids who hang out at the store. He's a bit
of a hero, and the waitresses perk up as he comes in*

Chuck Yo, Mr C!
Mr Cohen Yeah, yeah, morning Chuck. (*He goes back to reading his
newspaper*)
Joey Yo, Chuck!
Chuck (*teasing Joey*) Who said that?
Waitresses Mr Nobody! (*They giggle*)
Chuck Morning Cherry, Peaches, Pumpkin, Honey.
Waitresses (*dreamily*) Morning Chuck.

The customers greet each other

Dirk Manley (*narrating*) Chuck and his gang used to hang out at the
ice-cream parlour. He was always pickin' on poor old Joey. Yep, just
another day at Uncle Angelo's.

All (*singing*) It's just another day, hanging round the store,
Another day, no different than before.
The sodas flow with Uncle Angelo
Uh-o uh-o
Poodle skirts, ponytails a-swishin'.
All the guys for Thunderbirds are wishin'.
Don't drive slow to Uncle Angelo,
Uh-o uh-o
Summer's hot, we gotta keep the temp'rature low.
Uncle Angelo's is the place to go!
Uh-o
A-whoa whoa whoa whoa
Rockin'and a-rollin' in our saddle shoes
The neatest way to beat the summer blues.
We go, go, go to Uncle Angelo
Uh-o uh-o
We go, go, go to Uncle Angelo!
Uncle Angelo!

The customers talk quietly, and the waitresses take down orders from the customers

*[optional] American street sounds, cars and footsteps, etc. are heard, creating low atmospherics in the backround.This track can be raised briefly every time the "door"is opened throughout the show, and must be faded out for each song

Dirk Manley (*narrating*) That week had started out just like any other...

Chuck throws his baseball cap at a coat hook on the wall, but the hook is broken and the cap falls to the floor

Chuck Hey Joey! When you gonna fix that hook, huh? It's been busted for years!
Joey I'll do it right now, Chuck!

Joey rushes over towards the hook, but the waitresses distract him as they move DS *to give him their orders. He runs to each girl to collect the orders*

Cherry Hey Joey! We need three vanilla colas ——
Peaches — two Angelo's Delights ——
Pumpkin — a cheeseburger with everything on it ——
Honey — and a pretzel!

Joey Sure thing, girls! Two vanilla colas, a special, three bacon burgers and a peanut, coming up!
Waitresses (*exasperated*) Joey!
Cherry Three colas ——
Peaches — two specials ——
Pumpkin — one burger ——
Honey — with cheese!
Waitresses And a pretzel!
Joey Got it! Err — I think.
Mr Cohen Joey! Clean up that mess! (*He points to the bar*)

Joey starts to go over to the bar

Joey Yes, sir, right away, sir!
Chuck Joey! The hook?!
Joey I'll get to it, Chuck, I promise!

As the dialogue continues, in the background a customer puts a coin in the jukebox and pushes a button

*The sound of an American street fades

No. 1a Will He Find Me? (on cassette)

The jukebox begins to play beneath the dialogue

Joey hastily tidies up, and then begins to put the orders out on four trays on the bar for the waitresses

The customer returns to his/her seat

Customer (*to a friend, as he/she sits back down from the jukebox*) This jukebox only ever plays one song! I'm fed up of hearing, "Will He Find Me?".
Customer We need some rock and roll!
Customer Elvis Presley
Customer Bill Haley!
Mr Cohen I'll get Joey to fix it one of these days.
Waitresses We like this song!

The music should get a little louder as the waitresses sing along with the chorus

Waitresses (*singing*) Will he find me?
                Will he find me?
                When will he find me?

They stop singing as Joey puts the orders out on the bar and calls to them

The music fades down to background level as the dialogue continues

Joey Here ya go, ladies! Mr Cohen, can I talk to you about something, please?

The waitresses collect their trays and deliver the orders as Joey speaks to Mr Cohen

Mr Cohen Joey, I gave you a pay raise a year ago. Waddya want, *more* money, already?
Joey Oh no, sir, it's about my brand new sooper-dooper ice-cream flavour —
Mr Cohen (*overlapping*) — ice-cream flavour. I already told ya, Joey. I can't afford for you to be wasting time in the stock room inventing sooper-dooper anything! We got enough on our hands trying to keep these customers happy.
Joey I know, sir, but —

As Mr Cohen speaks, he walks across the stage. Joey follows closely behind him, mirroring his steps

Mr Cohen No buts! That new place, Crazy Flavours, has just about taken all my customers away. If they open up *another* Crazy Flavours, we ain't gonna have no customers at all.

Mr Cohen stops suddenly, and Joey almost crashes into the back of him

Joey But, sir —
Mr Cohen And if you don't get back to work, you ain't gonna have no job at all! Do I make myself perfectly clear?
Joey Yes, sir.
Waitresses Poor old Mr Nobody! (*They giggle*)
Chuck Hey girls, go easy on Joey! I bet his sooper-dooper ice-cream flavour would be bigger than baseball!
Customer Nothin's bigger than baseball!
Chuck (*leaping on to a chair*) I can just see it now — "Nobody's Ice-Cream Parlour."

Everyone laughs, and Joey looks a little sad

*If the jukebox hasn't finished playing, it should be faded out completely for
the song*

Mr Cohen Hey! Get offa the furniture!
Chuck Cool it, Mr C! Ya know, we're your best customers!
Mr Cohen You're my *only* customers!
Chuck But we just *love* your flavours!

The Lights cross-fade to a general blue full-stage wash, with a spot on Chuck

No. 2 Shake, Ripple & Roll

(*Singing*) We'll come in here so long as you
Keep servin' all the things you do
'Cause there ain't nothin' I could dream ——

The Lights change to rock and roll style: bright colours and flashing lights

	(*Speaking*) — that's cooler, smoother
	Sweeter, neater,
	Slicker, quicker than ice-cream!
	(*Singing*) Well there is somethin' 'bout vanilla
	In a chillin' sarsaparilla of a shake
All	Shake shake
	Shake shake
Chuck	And choc'late is so neat
	It's a real candy treat in a shake
All	Shake shake
	Shake shake
Chuck	Cherry cola is a dream
	When you add the Dairy Queen for a shake
All	Shake, Ripple and Roll!
	Shake, Ripple and Roll!
Chuck	We wanna ——
All	Shake, Ripple and Roll!
Chuck	Yeah baby ——
All	Shake, Ripple and Roll!
	There ain't nothin' to it
	All the kids'll wanna do it
	Have a Shake, Ripple and Roll!

Chuck	It's a real wild ride
	With a pretzel on the side of a shake
All	Shake shake
	Shake shake
Chuck	And the soda is so fizzy
	That the bubbles make you dizzy in a shake
All	Shake shake
	Shake shake
Chuck	So don't wait a minute later
	Open up the Kelvinator for a shake
All	Shake, Ripple and Roll!
	Shake, Ripple and Roll!
Chuck	We wanna ——
All	Shake, Ripple and Roll!
Chuck	Yeah baby ——
All	Shake, Ripple and Roll!
	There ain't nothin' to it
	All the kids'll wanna do it
	Have a Shake, Ripple and Roll!

Dance break

Chuck	If you're in the candy mood
	You can be the coolest dude with a shake
All	Shake shake
	Shake shake
Chuck	If you really got the lick
	You can be the hippest chick with a shake
All	Shake shake
	Shake shake
Chuck	So don't walk on by
	Won't ya come on in and try a little shake
All	Shake, Ripple and Roll!
	Shake, Ripple and Roll!
Chuck	We wanna ——
All	Shake, Ripple and Roll!
Chuck	Yeah baby——
All	Shake, Ripple and Roll
	There ain't nothin' to it
	All the kids'll wanna do it
	Have a Shake, Ripple and Roll!

All   There ain't nothin' to it
                      All the kids'll wanna do it
                      Have a shake ——
Chuck   (*speaking*) Shake shake!
All   (*singing*) Ripple and Roll!

*The Lights cross-fade to general bright full-stage wash. * The sound of an
American street and footsteps etc. is heard*

*Everyone returns to their chairs/stools and chats quietly. Joey cleans glasses
with a white tea-towel and the waitresses return to serving the customers*

Dirk Manley (*narrating*) Everybody was kinda happy that day. Until the
phone rang…

The phone rings (on cassette)

Mr Cohen goes to answer the telephone

Mr Cohen Uncle Angelo's…. Oh, hallo…. Oh no! … When? … How? …
He said what? … So. … Oh, OK. … Yeah, thanks. … G'bye. (*He hangs
up the phone and walks towards Joey, looking sad*)
Joey Gee, Mr Cohen, you look awfully pale. You OK?
Mr Cohen That was Mr Lions.
Joey Of Lions, Tigers and Bears?
Waitresses Oh my!
Mr Cohen Yeah, Uncle Angelo's lawyer. Joey, girls, I got some bad news.

*The four waitresses and Joey crowd around Mr Cohen. Some of the
customers overhear the next part, and spread the word quietly in the
background until everyone knows*

Waitresses What is it, Mr Cohen?
Mr Cohen It's Uncle Angelo. He's gone.
Cherry ⎱ (*together*) Gone on vacation?
Peaches ⎰
Mr Cohen No — *gone.*
Honey ⎱ (*together*) Gone fishin' ?
Pumpkin ⎰
Mr Cohen No no, no. *Gone.* Gone to the greatest ice-cream parlour of them
all.
Waitresses He's gone to *Crazy Flavours*?
Joey I think Mr Cohen means that Uncle Angelo has ——

Joey and Mr Cohen take off their hats

—passed away.

Cherry Ooohhh ...

Peaches You ——

Pumpkin — mean ——

Honey — he's ——

Waitresses — dead?!

The waitresses burst into loud tears. Joey and Mr Cohen put their hats back on. Mr Cohen doesn't quite know how to deal with crying girls, so he moves away to the bar

Joey Don't cry, girls!

Mr Cohen It gets worse.

Joey and the girls move over to Mr Cohen

Uncle Angelo didn't leave no will.

Joey Are you sure?

Customer What's a will?

Joey It's a piece of paper sayin' who gets your stuff after you die.

Customer What stuff did Uncle Angelo have?

Mr Cohen ⎫ (*together*) This place.

Joey ⎭

Customer Oh!

Customer So who gets to own Uncle Angelo's, now that there ain't no Uncle Angelo?

Customer Yeah, and what are we gonna call it?

Mr Cohen As far as I know, Uncle Angelo ain't got no family, so there ain't no next of kin.

Customer Next of which?

Joey It means closest relative.

*The sounds of an American street fade out for the song

Cherry Poor Uncle Angelo.

Peaches He had no family ——

Pumpkin — and now that he's gone ——

Honey — he doesn't even have us any more.

The Lights cross-fade to a general blue full-stage wash with individual shafts of white heavenly light. There is a spot on Mr Cohen

No. 3 Angelo's An Angel Now

Mr Cohen	Poor Angelo
All	Doo da doo da doo da doo
Mr Cohen	It was his time to go
All	Doo da doo da doo da doo
Mr Cohen	Now he's flown up on high
All	Doo da doo da doo da doo
Mr Cohen	To serve ice cream in the sky
All	Ba ba ba, ba ba ba
	Ba ba ba, ba ba ba ba!

Mr Cohen	He's standing proud
All	Doo da doo da doo da doo
Mr Cohen	On a little white cloud
All	Doo da doo da doo da doo
Mr Cohen	And now he can boast
All	Doo da doo da doo da doo
Mr Cohen	He serves the heavenly host
All	Ba ba ba, ba ba ba,
	Ba ba ba, ba ba ba ba!

Mr Cohen	We miss our dear old uncle	**All**	Ahh...
	But, on the other hand,		Ooo...
	We know that he'll be happy		Ahh...
	Up in the promised land		Ooo...
	Where soda fountains gush with		Ahh...
	The nectar of the Lord,		Ooo...
	And there's a glow		Bop bop
	Beneath the flow		Bop bop
	Of every shake that's poured!		Shoobidy doobidy
			doo

Mr Cohen	He'll make the most
All	Doo da doo da doo da doo
Mr Cohen	Outta bein'a ghost
All	Doo da doo da doo da doo
Mr Cohen	His faithful soul
All	Doo da doo da doo da doo
Mr Cohen	Sellin' clouds by the bowl
All	Ba ba ba, ba ba ba,
	Ba ba ba, ba ba ba!

Mr Cohen	So say goodbye
All	Doo da doo da doo da doo
Mr Cohen	As he meets them on high
All	Doo da doo da doo da doo
Mr Cohen	They'll be sayin' hallo
All	Doo da doo da doo da doo
Mr Cohen	To Uncle Angelo.
All	Doo da doo da doo da doo
Mr Cohen	They'll be sayin' hallo
All	Doo da doo da doo da doo
Mr Cohen	To Uncle Angel—— (*Pronounced like the word "angel"*)
All	Oh...

The Lighting cross-fades to a general bright stage wash

The customers sit back down again, leaving the main characters to talk

*The sound of an American street, cars and footsteps etc. is heard

Joey What are we gonna do, Mr Cohen?

Mr Cohen I dunno, Joey. Uncle Angelo used to say that if anything ever happened to him, this place'd be in good hands. But if he ain't left a will——

Joey What if he *did* leave a will?

Mr Cohen Joey, don't be ridiculous.

Chuck Hey, Mr C, wouldn't he leave the place to you?

Mr Cohen Sure, Chuck, I guess he would. But without a will the lawyers might decide to sell the place.

Cherry But ——

Peaches — what's gonna happen ——

Pumpkin — to us ——

Honey — if this place closes?

Mr Cohen You girls could get a job someplace else. But I don't know what'd happen to me. And Joey lives here. He ain't got no other place to go.

Joey I'll be OK, sir. Don't worry about me. Didn't Uncle Angelo say anything about all this before he died?

Mr Cohen His last words were: "Will He Find Me?"

Chuck The name of the song on the jukebox? Why would he say that?

Customer Maybe he liked that song?

Mr Cohen Yeah, maybe. OK everybody, back to work. We can't do anything until tomorrow.

The Lighting cross-fades to a dim blue general wash. A special comes up on Dirk Manley

*The sound of an American street fades out

Dirk Manley (*narrating*) Mr Cohen didn't sleep good that night. In fact, everybody was worried. Would Uncle Angelo's have to close? What would happen to Joey if it did? Why didn't Uncle Angelo leave a will, or had he left one somewhere in the store? Why would he say the name of a jukebox song before he died? Why am I asking you?

*The sound of an American street is heard

The next day, things got even worse.

Everybody switches places, freezing in a tableau to indicate that it is now the following day. At this point, a new group of chorus can be used if required

The Lights cross-fade to a general bright full-stage wash

They'd just opened up when a lady walked through the door...

Deanna la Domme, a movie star, appears at the door and poses. She is dripping with diamonds and furs. Her timid chauffeur, Max, is standing beside her. He is carrying her small evening purse and her small dog

*The sound of the American street becomes a little louder as Deanna la Domme enters, to indicate that the door is open

No-one has noticed Deanna la Domme enter so she nudges Max. He clears his throat loudly. The four waitresses are the first to notice

*The sound of the American street quietens

Waitresses Oh my goodness! It's Deanna la Domme, the movie star!
Dirk Manley (*narrating*) It was Deanna la Domme, the movie star.
Customer Deanna la Domme, the movie star?
Dirk Manley (*narrating*) Is there an echo in here?
Customer Oh-boy-oh-boy! (*He races over to Deanna*) Miss la Domme, I just *loved* you in "Revenge of the Wicked Witch".

Everyone rushes over to Deanna la Domme to get her autograph, except Joey and Mr Cohen, who hover by the bar

Dirk Manley (*narrating*) Deanna la Domme was a movie star, all right, but she hadn't made a movie in a long time.
Customer (*to a friend*) She's so beautiful, ain't she?
Dirk Manley (*narrating*) She was beautiful, there ain't no denying it.

As Joey goes to follow the crowd, Mr Cohen stops him

Joey But I want to get Miss la Domme's autograph!
Mr Cohen Joey, I smell trouble.

During the following Deanna la Domme disentangles herself from the crowd and makes her way into the store

Joey You think the grill caught fire again?
Mr Cohen No, no, no. Answer me this: why would Deanna la Domme the movie star come into Uncle Angelo's, huh?
Joey Maybe she wants an ice-cream?
Mr Cohen Joey, Joey, Joey, one of these days ...
Chuck Miss la Domme, please, have my seat.
Deanna Such a sweet offer, but I'm looking for the manager. Is he here?
Customer That's him, over there.
Mr Cohen I'm the manager, lady. What can I do for you? A soda, maybe?

Deanna walks over to Mr Cohen

Deanna I'm afraid I'm here on a rather more serious matter than silly old ice cream.
Customer (*aside to the waitresses*) Did she just say "silly old ice-cream"?
Waitresses (*aside to Customer*) Uh-huh.
Deanna As you may have heard, Angelo is ... (*She starts to sob back tears dramatically*) Angelo has...

Deanna clicks her fingers at Max, who desperately searches in her small evening purse for a handkerchief. Chuck rushes over with a serviette and hands it to Deanna. Max gives Chuck an angry glare

Chuck Here you go, ma'am.
Deanna Oh — (*She hiccups*) Thank you. (*She wipes away a crocodile tear and continues*) Angelo passed away and ... and ... I shall miss my beloved uncle so *much* ...

Deanna breaks down, sobbing. Max desperately searches the evening purse again

Mr Cohen Wait a minute, wait a minute! Did you say *your* uncle?
Deanna Oh, didn't you know? Dear, sweet Uncle Angelo was mother's half-brother. I shall feel his absence... We were very close. Weren't we, Max? Max!!
Max (*looking up from the evening purse*) Yes, ma'am!
Mr Cohen (*muttering*) He ain't never mentioned you to me.
Deanna (*snaps*) He was very private about it. The fact of the matter *is*, Mr Cohen, that Uncle Angelo wanted *me* to have this — (*disdainfully*) — place when he died.

Deanna hands the used serviette to Max, who hands it to Joey, who pulls a disgusted face

I'm afraid you'll have to close down at the end of the week.
Joey Close down?!

Everyone reacts with surprise and dismay to this news

Deanna I shall be selling it ——

She pauses for everyone to show surprise

— to Crazy Flavours.
Mr Cohen Now wait just one cotton-pickin' minute! You got any *proof* that Uncle Angelo left this place to you? A will, maybe?
Deanna Alas — (*she sobs*) — dear Uncle Angelo never had the chance to make out a will. His death was so — (*with a little menacing pride*) — sudden. But as his only living relative, I have the claim to his property. And I have a letter here from his lawyer, to say so.

She snaps her fingers at Max, who takes a letter out of her evening purse and gives it to Mr Cohen. Deanna and Max move away from everyone else

Customer Wassit say, Mr Cohen?
Mr Cohen Well, she's right, I'm afraid. Unless we can find a will, Uncle Angelo's belongs to her.

Deanna and Max stand DS *and speak out of earshot of everyone else*

Deanna You *did* remember to burn every copy of the will, didn't you, Max?
Max Yes, ma'am.
Deanna Good boy.

Deanna and Max do not hear the next section of dialogue, until the song begins. She looks in an imaginary mirror on the "fourth wall". Max hands her a lipstick from her evening purse and she touches up her make-up as the others talk

Joey What are we gonna do, Mr Cohen?
Customer It's a real shame there ain't no will.
Joey But ... what if there is?
Mr Cohen Joey, Uncle Angelo didn't even have no bank account. He never trusted nobody 'cept me with his money.
Joey So maybe he left his will with you!?
Mr Cohen But I don't *have* it. Joey! Wassamatter with your head today? You ain't thinkin' straight, Mr Nobody.
Joey I know. I was gonna say maybe he hid it in the store, but ——
Mr Cohen Quiet, Joey, I'm thinkin'. (*He pauses*) I got an idea! Maybe he hid it in the store! Wow, I'm a genius.

*The sound of an American street fades out for the song

Joey But where would he hide it?
Mr Cohen She said we had a week, right? We'll find it.
Joey What happens if we *don't* find it?
Mr Cohen We're doomed.

The Lights cross-fade to a general bright orange and yellow wash, with a spot on Mr Cohen and Deanna

No. 4 Where There's a Will

Mr Cohen   Where there's a will, there's gonna be a way
                      To prove the lady is a fake.
                      We only got a week to look, but hey!
                      A piece of cake!

Deanna   Oh Uncle Angelo,
                      Why did you have to go?
                      My poor heart will break in two,
                      And now I seem to find
                      That everything reminds me of you.

Mr Cohen   Who does she think she's kidding anyhow?
                      What is the drama all about?
                      If Uncle Angelo could be here now,
                      He'd throw her out!

Deanna   You know it makes me weep
To think I cannot keep
Uncle Angelo's delight,
But I will stand up tall
And face each day with all of my might.

Dance break

Mr Cohen ⎫
Half Chorus ⎭
  Where there's a will
  There's gonna be a way—
  To prove the lady is a fake.
  We only have a week to look
  But hey! —
  A piece of cake!
  Who does she think
  She's kidding anyhow?—
  What is the drama all about?
  If Uncle Angelo could be here now
  He'd throw her out!

Deanna ⎫
Half Chorus ⎭
  Oh Uncle Angelo,
  Why did you have to go? —
  My poor heart will break —
    in two,
  And now I seem to find
  That everything reminds me
    of you.
  You, know it makes me weep
  To think I cannot keep—
  Uncle Angelo's delight,
  But I will stand up tall —
  And face each day with all
    of my might.

Dance break

During the dance break Deanna takes Max's buttonhole rose and dances with it between her teeth

The Lights cross-fade to a general bright full-stage wash

*The sound of an American street can be crept back in at this point

Deanna begins to sob again

Deanna The funeral is on Friday — (*She snaps out of sobbing*) So you have until Saturday to leave. (*Her sobbing resumes*) I'm so sorry. (*Her sobbing ends abruptly*) Come on, Max. We're leaving.
Max Yes, ma'am.
Mr Cohen Well, ain't *she* the friendly one!
Chuck What are you gonna do, Mr C?
Mr Cohen Don't you worry. I'll think 'a somethin'.

Deanna and Max move to the door, out of earshot of the others

Deanna I thought my performance was Oscar material, didn't you?
Max Oh yes, ma'am, absolutely.

The Light slow-fade to night-time interior, with a special on Dirk Manley

The customers exit during the following narration

Mr Cohen, Joey and the four waitresses are left alone in the store. It is the end of the day

*The sound of an American street should fade out at this point

During the following, the waitresses are cleaning up the store: sweeping with a dustpan and brush, putting glasses on the bar and dusting with a feather duster or white tea towels. Joey is sweeping with his broom and Mr Cohen is sorting out the cash register

Dirk Manley (*narrating*) It looked like Deanna la Domme had got 'em good. The lawyer's letter confirmed that she was Uncle Angelo's only living relative. Unless they could come up with the will by the end of the week, she'd sell the place to Crazy Flavours. Had Deanna's chauffeur burned every copy, or had Uncle Angelo left one secret copy in the store? Just as they were closing up for the night, Mr Cohen came up with a good plan.

The special on Dirk Manley fades

Mr Cohen (*coming over to Joey and pulling him to one side*) Joey, I got a good plan.
Joey What is it, sir?
Mr Cohen Spend the rest of the night searching the store for the will.
Joey I'll search all night if I have to!
Mr Cohen You're a good kid, Joey, no matter what they say. Ya know, I don't trust that Deanna la Domme one little bit.
Joey Maybe you should get her checked out, sir?
Mr Cohen Checked out, checked out, sheesh, you're making this sound like a detective movie.
Joey (*quietly, almost to himself*) Well, that's kinda what I meant...
Mr Cohen A detective! Yeah, now there's an idea! Joey, where do I find a private investigator?
Joey Err... in the phone directory, under ——

Mr Cohen — under P! Joey...

Mr Cohen turns to Joey and takes his hand, as if to shake it. Joey obviously thinks that Mr Cohen is going to thank him, and he looks very proud and happy

Joey Yes, sir?!
Mr Cohen I'm a genius!

Mr Cohen marches offstage, leaving Joey with his hand still outstretched, his smile gone

Joey (*sadly, to the air that was Mr Cohen a moment before*) Yes, sir.

Peaches, Pumpkin, Cherry and Honey pile their dusting cloths into Joey's hands as they talk to him

Cherry Hey Joey, ain't you worried about the store closin' down?
Peaches Yeah, Joey, where you gonna go?
Joey Sure I'm worried, ladies. I guess I'll have to get another job.
Pumpkin But you live here, Joey. You got any family you can stay with?
Joey (*sadly*) I don't remember, Pumpkin.
Honey (*to Pumpkin*) He ain't got no memory, bubble head! Why d'ya think we call him Joey Nobody?
Pumpkin Oh yeah, I forgot.

Pause

Peaches You forgot that he forgot!

The waitresses giggle

Joey (*a little angry*) You just wait and see! Someday I'm gonna have my memory back, and then I'll have a real name, and a family, and a home, and— and——
Cherry And what?
Peaches Yeah, Joey, I mean, what can you do 'cept for makin' ice-cream sodas?

Joey looks wounded for a moment

Joey (*defiant*) Maybe I'll have my own ice-cream joint one day.

Pumpkin Oh yeah, Mr Nobody. Maybe Uncle Angelo left this place to —
(*she pauses for effect*) — you!

The waitresses giggle again

Honey "Mr Nobody's Ice-Cream Parlour"! Just like Chuck said!
Waitresses Chuck is *so* dreamy.

*The Lights slow fade to a very dark blue general wash. A small spot comes
up on Joey*

*The waitresses start to chatter amongst themselves as they turn suddenly
and leave the store*

*Joey doesn't realize they are going until they have gone. He turns and races
after them, shouting*

Joey Oh, good-night, ladies! (*He sadly realizes he's alone*) Maybe someday
they'll say that about me. Ahh, who am I kidding? I'll never be like Chuck.
I'll always be me. Whoever that is. (*He sings*)

No. 5 Nobody's Lament

I'm Nobody.
If you should ever look
Then you'd see Nobody.
I could write a book
About the way that people stare
As if I wasn't there, because

I'm Nobody.
Some folk got lots of fam'ly.
I got Nobody.
Whenever I get lonely
On a starry summer night,
Who holds my hand too tight?
Nobody.

Who could own a store that's
The size of all New York?
Nobody could, Nobody could.
Who would give a job to all
The people out of work?

Nobody would, Nobody would.
Who should be a hero,
And not a soda jerk?
Nobody should, Nobody should!

I'm Nobody!
It may be hard to see me,
But I'm Nobody!
Someday they'll wanna be me
As I stand up straight and proud
And shout my name out loud!
I'm——

Mr Cohen (*offstage, speaking*) Don't forget to sweep the floor, Joey.
Joey (*singing meekly*) — Nobody.

The Lights slowly come up to a general bright full-stage wash

During the following narration, the company come back into the store, ready for the next scene. At this point, a new group of chorus can be used if required. Joey goes over to the broken coat hook and fixes it quickly

*The sound of an American street is heard

Dirk Manley (*narrating*) Joey looked for the will all night, but he didn't find anything. (*He walks over to the "door" as he speaks, for he is the person entering*) The next day, as the customers started strollin' in, a new guy showed up.

From this point onwards, some of Dirk Manley's speech is dialogue delivered to the other characters, and some is narration delivered to the audience

(*Narrating*) This was one very cool dude. Yeah, it was me. Cohen had called me the night before, and I told him I'd take the case. A movie star, a lost will, a dead uncle ——

Two waitresses cross the stage in front of him as they go to take orders from some customers

Cute chicks. As much free ice-cream as I could eat. How could I say no? Naturally, I showed up in disguise. I didn't wanna scare the customers.

He removes his coat to reveal a garish shirt and long, brightly-coloured shorts. He slicks back his hair and chews non-existent gum. A few customers notice him at this moment and gasp loudly. Dirk looks at them and then glares at the audience. Mr Cohen looks up and sees him

Mr Cohen (*loudly*) Can I take your coat, sir? (*Hissing*) You were supposed to be in disguise!

Dirk Manley (*hissing back*) I *am* in disguise. Dirk Manley, Private Detective. Here's my card.

Dirk pulls a banana out of his pocket and hands it to Cohen, who takes it and pulls a puzzled face at the audience. Dirk notices the banana and pulls a card out of his hat-band

Oh. Here's my card. who are you?

Mr Cohen Cohen. I'm the manager.

Dirk Manley (*narrating*) I knew who he was. I was just making sure *he* knew.

Mr Cohen Err — great disguise. You'll really blend in with the bubblegum machine.

Dirk Manley Don't talk to me, don't talk to me. I'm working.

Mr Cohen She ain't here yet.

Dirk Manley Who?

Mr Cohen Deanna la Domme, the lady I hired you to check out.

Dirk Manley (*narrating*) I knew that, too,

Customer (*looking at the audience to see who Dirk has been talking to*) Hey, who are ya talkin' to?

Dirk Manley (*embarrassed*) Nobody.

Joey What?

Dirk Manley What?

Mr Cohen What?

Dirk Manley Get me an ice-cream, Cohen.

Customer Hey, I'll have an ice-cream, Cohen!

Customer Yeah, I'll have an ice-cream, Cohen!

Customer I'll have an ice-cream sundae!

Mr Cohen We might not *be* here Sunday!

Mr Cohen sighs and shakes his head, and goes to the bar to fetch an ice-cream cone for Dirk. The waitresses bustle around serving everyone else. Joey is behind the bar, and hands Mr Cohen an ice-cream cone

Joey (*to Mr Cohen*) Who's the guy dressed like a Tropical Sunrise?

Chuck Hey! It's Dirk Manley, the Private Detective!
Cherry Hi, Dirk!
Peaches Hey, Dirk!
Pumpkin Hallo, Dirk!
Honey Hiya, Dirk!

The waitresses giggle. Mr Cohen hands Dirk the ice-cream

Mr Cohen I thought you said nobody would recognize you?
Dirk Manley It's all part of my plan.

* *The sound of an American street should fade out at this point*

Mr Cohen Well, you coulda chosen a better disguise, that's all I'm sayin'.
But then, it's your case.
Dirk Manley It's my case? I knew that. Listen, buddy, I been in the detective
business for —— (*he counts on fingers*) — a real long time, OK? I am the
King of Undercover!

*The Lighting changes to rock and roll style: bright colours and flashing
lights. There is a spot on Dirk Manley. *The sound of the American street
fades down for the song*

*Dirk can use his ice-cream cone as a "microphone" if he is not using a real
hand-held mic for this song*

No. 6 Undercover Blues

Dirk Manley	If I'm in the jungle or in the street,
	You won't see me move, you won't hear my feet.
	I'm the man that you just can't lose,
	But uh-oh baby, I got some news…
	It's lonely,
	Livin' the way I do-o.
	Well, it's a cryin' shame,
	I got the Undercover Blues.
All	Blue, blue, bloo-oo-oo!
Dirk Manley	Uh huh huh
All	Blue, blue, bloo-oo-oo!
Dirk Manley	Well, I been like this since I was a kid,
	Always undercover, whatever I did.
	I met my mama when school was done,
	She said, "Uh uh, boy, you ain't my son"

It's lonely,
Livin' the way I do-o.
Well, it's a cryin' shame,
I got the Undercover Blues.
All   Blue, blue, bloo-oo-oo!
Dirk Manley Uh huh huh
All   Blue, blue, bloo-oo-oo!
Dirk Manley (*speaking*) Play it!

Dance break

Dirk Manley (*singing*) You can run from me but you just can't hide
'Cos wherever you go, I'll be by your side.
Look for me until the day is through,
But, oh yeah baby I'm foll'win' you.

It's lonely,
Livin' the way I do-o.
Well it's a cryin' shame,
I got the Undercover Blues.
All   Blue, blue, bloo-oo-oo!
Dirk Manley Uh huh huh
All   Blue, blue, bloo-oo-oo!
Dirk Manley Well it's a cryin' shame,
I got the Undercover Blues.
All   Blue, blue, bloo-oo-oo!
Dirk Manley Uh huh huh
All   Blue, blue, bloo-oo-oo!
Dirk Manley Well it's a cryin' shay — yay — yame ...
(*speaking*) Whoo!
(*singing*) I got the Undercover Blues.
All (*speaking*) Whoo! / Take it home, Brother! / Yeah! / All right! (*Other lines can be improvised, but all should be spoken at the same time, and all should be very brief*)
Dirk Manley (*singing*) Oh, yeah!

*The Lights cross-fade to a general bright full-stage wash. *The street sounds can be crept back in at this point*

Dirk Manley So, ya just let me know when she gets here, and I'll handle the rest.
Mr Cohen She's Deanna la Domme, the movie star.
Dirk Manley I knew that.

Mr Cohen Donchya think you'll recognize her?
Dirk Manley Yeah, but will you?

As Dirk Manley narrates, the customers and waitresses move away, Joey goes back behind the bar, and Mr Cohen sits on a bar stool to read his paper. Joey places the newspaper with the eye-hole on the bar

(*Narrating*) I knew that I'd have this case cracked the minute the lady walked through the door. I ain't dumb.

He puts his ice-cream into his shirt pocket, upside down. Realizing what he's just done, he removes it and pulls a face. Handing the cone to Joey, he sits on a bar stool next to Mr Cohen, picks up the eye-hole newspaper and opens it up so the audience can see his eyes

Deanna la Domme enters with Max

Dirk spots her and his jaw drops to the floor with his paper. He is frozen with shock and admiration. The customers and waitresses observe her entrance and talk quietly about her

Deanna What a lovely morning it is. Find me a chair, Max.
Max Yes, ma'am!
Dirk Manley She... she... she...!
Deanna Good-morning, Mr Cohen. I do hope you're well.
Mr Cohen Considerin' I ain't gonna have no job at the end of the week, I'm doin' just fine, *Miss la Domme*. (*He punctuates her name with three digs in Dirk's ribs*)
Deanna I'm so glad to hear that.

Max has pulled up a chair for her, but she sees dirt on the seat

(*Pointing to the chair*) Max!
Max Yes, ma'am! (*He cleans the dirt off with his pocket handkerchief*)
Dirk Manley She's Deanna la Domme, the movie star!
Mr Cohen (*moving over to Dirk*) I *knew* that! What are you waitin' for?

Mr Cohen pushes Dirk towards Deanna. Dirk kneels beside her chair, gazing up with adoration

Dirk Manley Miss la Domme, I've heard so much about you, and I just loved you in "Revenge of the Wicked Witch". Sign your autograph on the back of my business card, would you? I'd be so grateful, ma'am.

Mr Cohen and Joey are at the bar, away from Deanna and Dirk

Mr Cohen (*to Joey*) Can you hear what they're sayin'?
Joey (*listening*) Nope.
Mr Cohen Gee, I sure hope he gets the low-down before it's too late.

Deanna la Domme notices the name on his card as she signs her autograph. She hands the card back, and as Dirk is reading it, she turns to whisper to Max

Deanna (*to Max*) His card says he's a Private Detective. So, they're spying on me, are they? We'll see about that! (*She turns back to Dirk Manley*) I hope you don't mind my asking, but do tell me about yourself. You look so — interesting.

Dirk Manley gulps, and turns to the audience

The Lighting snaps to a general blue full-stage wash. There is a spot on Dirk Manley. *The street sounds fade out

The company freezes as Dirk speaks aside

Dirk Manley (*narrating*) Of course, she couldn't resist my charms, and I could see that she was on the straight and narrow. Personally, I couldn't figure out why they didn't like her. Meanwhile, Mr Cohen was frettin' about the will ...

The Lighting snaps to general bright full stage wash. The spot fades on Dirk

Everyone comes to life again

Mr Cohen You didn't find *anything*, Joey?
Joey Not one thing, sir, and I looked all night. I did get that coat hook fixed, though!
Mr Cohen Joey, if the store closes down, who's gonna care about the coat hook?

A customer puts a coin in the jukebox

The sound effect version of **Will He Find Me?** (**FX** *on cassette*) *begins to play. The song is stuck on a scratch and keeps repeating the chorus over and over again*

Mr Cohen And now the jukebox has had it! That's *all* I need. (*He goes over to it and kicks it*)

The song snaps to silence

When's it all gonna *end*?

The Lighting snaps to open-white footlights and a general blue wash

A member of the chorus stands up, in a suspension of disbelief moment, and sings to the audience. Others follow suit, singing around the main characters, who freeze in the background. This song may be sung by a separate group of chorus and each part of the song can be sung by more than one person if required. This song has an alternative arrangement, which is simpler and requires fewer parts of harmony. Both options are in the vocal score

No. 7 Somethin' Strange Is Goin' On

Chorus Groups A and B

First part	Ooo…
Second part	Ooo …
Third part	Ooo
Fourth part	Ooo …
5 parts	Wahhh!

All	When will it end?
	When will we know for sure?
	If the lady's no friend,
	We're gonna lose the store
	That we love
Group A	We love it so, but oh ——
All	Somethin' strange is goin' on.
Group B	Ba ba ba, ba ba ——
All	There's no doubt about it,
	We're up against a wall.
	And our ice-cream parlour
	Will soon become a mall —
	Full of folk
Group A	It ain't no joke
	Somethin' strange is goin' on.
Group B	Ba ba ba, ba ba ——

Group A We'll have to wait until   **Group B** Da doo da da doo
Someone finds the will   Da da doo da da doo
And then we can fulfil   Da doo da da doo da da doo
Our dream   Da da doo da da doo da
                                                             doo

All   To keep this little store —
                   Is what we're aimin' for,
                   But golly, wow
                   Ain't nothing now
                   Is actually how it seems ...

The Lights snap to bright red, white and blue full-stage wash

As Dirk Manley speaks, the cast move into their new positions for the next song

Deanna and Max exit. At this point, the customers can exit and a new group of chorus can be used. If Deanna's Boys are taken from the main chorus, they should leave the stage now in order to be able to enter with Deanna after No. 8 Today's the Day! They can make a costume change during that number if required

Dirk Manley (*narrating*) The rest of the week went too fast.

No.8 Today's the Day! *begins to underscore*

Mr Cohen and Joey looked everywhere for the will, but they didn't find nothing. Time was passin', and it sure looked like Cohen was gonna lose Uncle Angelo's.

                     No. 8 Today's the Day!

All (*singing*)   Wednesday's here already
                   And we ain't heard nothing yet.
                   By Saturday we'll have to pay
                   The dues upon the bet.
                   There ain't no sign of help around,
                   There ain't no second chance.
                   By Saturday we'll hear them say
                   "Let's do the final dance."
                   Wednesday here will disappear,
                   And then where do we get?
                   Another day has gone away,
                   Another sun has set.

                   Thursday's here already,
                   And we just ain't found a thing.
                   We're in a mess, an SOS,
                   And the days are gonna swing.
                   There ain't no-one can help us now,
                   There ain't no hope at all.
                   We're lookin' still, to find the will,

Won't someone hear our call?
Thursday's gonna fly and then
We don't have much more time.
Another day has gone away,
It really is a crime.

Friday's here already,
And tomorrow is the day
And we can hear the sound of fear
As the jungle drummers play.
They're beatin' out the rhythm
Of impending doom and gloom.
We're standin' by and wond'rin' why
The time is goin' zoom.
Friday's almost gone and then
You know what's on the way.

The hour is here, and now it's clear
That today's our Judgement Day.

Today's our Judgement Day
Today's our Judgement Day
Today's our Judgement Day
Today's our Judgement Day
It's Saturday... Today! Today! Today!
(*Speaking*) TODAY!

The Lighting cross-fades to a general bright full-stage wash

It's Saturday, the day that Deanna la Domme is due to take over the store.
Everyone resets themselves for the next scene

* *The American street sounds fade back in at this point*

Dirk Manley (*narrating*) It was Saturday, and they were no closer to a
solution. Deanna arrived in her limousine, all ready to collect the keys ...

Deanna, Max and Deanna's Boys enter. The boys can be played by a
separate group of chorus if required

The boys are carrying parcels from her shopping trip. Deanna is wearing a
fancy coat which she takes off and holds out to Mr Cohen as she enters. As

*she speaks, he takes it and walks over towards the coat hook. Deanna looks
away for a moment, and he purposefully drops it on the floor in a heap and
kicks it*

Deanna Well, Mr Cohen, I believe I gave you a week. You haven't done
much packing, I see. Never mind. The wreckers will just demolish the
place with everything in it, I should imagine. The keys, if you please.

*Cohen is still near the coat hook. Deanna holds out her hand, but he just folds
his arms and looks defiant*

Max, boys, help Mr Cohen find the keys to the store, would you?
Max Yes, ma'am!

*The boys all place their parcels into the arms of the very smallest boy, who
ends up with a pile of parcels taller than he is. He drops them all, looks guilty,
and piles them up out of the way as Max marches over to Mr Cohen. Max
holds out his hand, and the other boys line up behind him with their arms
folded. The smallest one runs to join them at the back of the line*

Mr Cohen You ain't havin' them.
Deanna Excuse me?

*The tallest boy picks Max up by the shoulders of his jacket, lifts him out of the
way and towers over Mr Cohen. Max runs behind the tall boy as he holds out
his hand for the keys*

Mr Cohen I said, you ain't havin' the keys.
Dirk Manley Now come on, Cohen. She's got proof of ownership, ya know.
You don't got much choice in the matter, buddy.
Mr Cohen Oh, great, now you're on *her* side? Sheesh.
Dirk Manley Ya can't fight the law, Cohen. If you ain't got a copy of Uncle
Angelo's will, Miss la Domme is the legal owner of this here ice-cream
parlour. I wish I could help ya.
Cherry Oh, no!
Peaches You just can't ——
Pumpkin — take away the store ——
Honey — Miss la Domme!
Deanna (*sighing impatiently*) Must you always speak together like that? It
gives me a headache.
Chuck Have you looked everywhere, Mr C?
Mr Cohen Everywhere.
Joey I've looked, too. We didn't find anything, Chuck.

Waitresses What are we gonna do?

Deanna Try realizing that you work for me now. And you're all fired.

The staff and customers react to this

The American Street sound fades out at this point. It is not used again

Joey (*to Dirk*) And she seemed so nice in the movies!

Dirk Uh huh.

Deanna Nice? Nice and a token will get you on the subway. Don't you know who I am? Tell 'em, boys.

The Lights snap to a red full-stage general wash, with a spot on Deanna

No. 9 Deanna

Max }
Boys }   (*chanting*) Deanna, Deanna, Star of the Screen,
                    Deanna, Deanna, the Movie Queen,
                    Deanna, Deanna, Star of the Show,
                    Deanna, we love her so!

Deanna (*singing*) I am Deanna the Queen of the Night.
                    You've never seen such a beautiful sight.
                    In all my movies I am the star.
                    There's no-one greater.
                    I'm the brightest one by far.

Max }
Boys }   (*chanting*)Deanna, Deanna, Star of the Show!
                    Deanna, we love her so!

Deanna (*singing*) If there's a part for a devilish dame,
                    They call on me, dear, for that is my game.
                    In all the greatest movies they show.
                    I'm the greatest
                    Star that you will ever know.

Max }
Boys }   (*chanting*) Deanna, Deanna, Star of the Show!
                    Deanna, we love her so!

Deanna (*singing*) I can play the sweetest lady,
                    Or the tramp without a dime,
                    But let me tell you, baby,
                    I'm at my best

Max⎱ (*chanting*) Keep all the rest!
Boys⎰
Deanna (*singing*) When the part involves a crime!
Max⎱ (*chanting*) Deanna, Deanna, Star of the Screen
Boys⎰   Deanna, Deanna, the Movie Queen,
                   Deanna, Deanna, Star of the Show,
                   Deanna, we love her so!

Deanna (*singing*) So darling, don't walk on by if we meet.
                   Show me respect as you fall at my feet.
                   I love to see my —
                   Fans as they crawl.
Max⎱ (*chanting*) Star of the Screen!
Boys⎰
Deanna (*singing*) Loved by all.
Max⎱ (*chanting*) Movie Queen!
Boys⎰
Deanna (*singing*) Belle of the Ball.
Max⎱ (*chanting*) Star of the Show.
Boys⎰
Deanna (*speaking*) Donchya just love me?
            (*Singing*) They love me so!   **Max**⎱ (*singing*) We love
                                    Boys⎰   you so!
Max⎱ (*speaking*) Deanna!
Boys⎰

The Lighting cross-fades to a general bright full-stage wash

Deanna turns to Mr Cohen

Deanna Now then, the keys, if you please.
Joey Wait a minute! What if Uncle Angelo had a secret copy of the will, and
    he hid it right here in this ice-cream parlour?
Mr Cohen Yeah!
Deanna (*with a mock sigh*) Very well. I am a reasonable person, Mr Cohen.
Mr Cohen (*muttering*) Ya could have fooled me.
Deanna Search the store.
Joey⎱ (*to the customers*) Search the store!
Mr Cohen⎰
Deanna You have one minute.
Joey⎱ (*to each other*) One minute?!
Mr Cohen⎰
Deanna Your time starts — now!

Joey
Mr Cohen } (*to the audience*) Argh!!

No. 10 The Will (Instrumental)

The music underscores the following dialogue

The Lighting snaps to open-white footlights only

Deanna, Max and her Boys stand motionless whilst the others run madly around the store, searching under tables and in cupboards, and even each other. They look everywhere

Mr Cohen Joey, look under the bar!
Joey I'm trying to!
Dirk Ow! Who stepped on my foot!
Chuck Did anyone try the stockroom?
Joey I looked there last night!
Mr Cohen Well look there again!

Joey begins to head out to the stockroom, but sees Deanna's coat on the floor

Joey Hey! Who left their coat on the floor? I fixed the hook!
Mr Cohen Joey, we don't have *time* for coat hooks!

Joey places the coat on the coat hook and as if by magic, the jukebox swings open to reveal a safe!

The Lighting snaps to a spot on the jukebox and general full-stage blue wash

Everyone stops in their tracks and gasps. Joey doesn't see the safe immediately

Mr Cohen Joey, look what you did!
Joey I'm sorry! (*Pause*) What did I do?
Mr Cohen You found a safe! No *wonder* the jukebox never worked!
Deanna (*aside*) Drat and double drat. (*To Mr Cohen*) You don't have the combination! And you only have twenty seconds left!
Joey What were Uncle Angelo's last words?
Mr Cohen The name of that dumb song, "Will he find me?"
Joey What's the number of the song?
Waitresses 54! It's our favourite song!
Joey Try that combination, quick!

Mr Cohen kneels by the safe and starts to turn the dial as Deanna counts down the last few seconds. As she counts, they manage to open the door of the safe. Inside it they find a copy of Uncle Angelo's will

This dialogue fits in very specifically with the music and must be spoken as indicated in the vocal score

Deanna Ten, nine, eight——
Mr Cohen It's working!
Deanna — seven, six, five ——
Mr Cohen A piece of paper!
Deanna — four, three, two ——
Mr Cohen It's the will!
Deanna (*starts to say "one", but it turns into...*) WHAT?! Give me that!

Deanna snatches the will from Mr Cohen and tries to run out of the door. She cannot find an escape route as she runs around

Mr Cohen Joey! Do something!

Joey runs forwards and collides with Deanna

The Lighting snaps to a general bright full stage wash

They both fall to the floor and in the confusion, Chuck grabs Deanna's hands and holds them behind her back. Mr Cohen grabs the will from her. Joey stays down on the floor, a little dazed. Max and Deanna's Boys look on in amazement

Deanna Let go of me, you horrible boy!
Chuck You're staying right where you are, Miss la Domme. Hey, Mr C ... wassit say?

Mr Cohen opens up the will and starts to read. As he reads, Joey slowly begins to get up

Mr Cohen (*reading aloud*) Being of sound mind...blah blah blah...I, Angelo Pucciniatti... blah blah blah ——

Mr Cohen scans through the will as others speak

Customer You OK, Joey?
Joey I feel a little — fuzzy...

Mr Cohen (*reading aloud*) — but my worldly possessions are few, and I leave them all to one person ——

All Who?!

Customer Joey, you look real pale.

Joey I think — that — my name's not Joey

Mr Cohen (*reading aloud*) — I have a son that no-one knows about. I didn't want him to end up like Papa, so I sent him away when he was just a kid, to live in a better neighbourhood with a good family. I leave everything I own to him.

Joey I think my name is ——

Mr Cohen (*reading aloud*) His name is ——

Joey   ⎱ (*together*) Angelino.
Mr Cohen ⎰

A shocked pause. Mr Cohen and Joey look at each other in surprise

Mr Cohen What did you say, Joey?

Joey (*slowly*) My name's not Joey. It's Angelino.

Waitresses But, that's the name in the will!

Mr Cohen Are *you* Uncle Angelo's son, Joey?

Joey Who, me? Nah. My parents lived in ... in ... Manhattan! Hey, I can remember where I lived!

Deanna Oh please! Don't try to pull a fast one on *me*! I know every trick in the book. (*Mocking*) "His name is Angelino". Nice try, Cohen, now lemme go and give me the keys to my store!

Deanna shakes Chuck off

Dirk Manley Deanna has a point, Cohen. What proof have you got? Joey got a bump on the head and now he got back his memory, but that ain't no proof he's the same Angelino.

Mr Cohen Wait, wait, there's more! (*Reading aloud*) "My son Angelino can be identified by a birthmark on his right arm, in the shape of an ice-cream cone!" Joey — roll up your right sleeve.

Joey rolls his sleeve up slowly, to reveal a birthmark, in the shape of an ice-cream cone.This should be painted on his upper arm as a large and colourful cartoon picture

Everyone gasps, and Joey looks at the audience in sudden realization

The music comes to an end

Cherry Oh my goodness.

Peaches Joey!
Pumpkin It's you!
Honey You're ——
Waitresses — Uncle Angelo's son!

The Lighting snaps to general dark blue wash, with a spot on Joey

Everyone but Joey freezes

No. 11 Nobody's Lament (Reprise)

Joey (*singing*)   Who could own a store
All of his own?
Nobody could, Nobody could.
Who would make his father
Proud of how he'd grown?
Nobody would, Nobody would.
Who should have a history,
A past that he has known?
Nobody should, Nobody should!

The Lighting snaps to a general bright full-stage wash

Everyone comes back to life

Cherry He's so brave!
Peaches And clever!
Pumpkin And talented!
Honey And handsome.

The waitresses sigh adoringly

Joey (*grinning from ear to ear*) Gee thanks, ladies.
Waitresses (*dreamily*) You're welcome, Angelino.
Deanna (*disgusted*) Oh, pa-leeze!
Mr Cohen Well, I'll be. Here ya go, Joey. I mean, Angelino. The keys to *your* store. Angelino's!

The customers, waitresses and Dirk cheer

Deanna (*trying to keep it together*) Of course, you'll never manage to stay open, not with the competition from Crazy Flavours.

Joey I've invented a brand new, sooper-dooper flavour of ice cream that no-one else sells. It'll be a hit, and everyone will have to come to Angelino's to buy it!

Deanna realizes that she has no hope left. She's lost, and they have won. Now she's desperate, and brings back the crocodile tears, which are almost real this time

Deanna But — what about me?
Dirk Manley Well, I guess I oughta take you to the police station, ma'am.
Deanna What have I done?! Max! Call me a lawyer!
Max You're a lawyer!
Deanna Max, call me a cab!
Max You're a cab!
Deanna Max, do something!

In desperation, Max improvises a very short tap dance routine, or something similar

Deanna Max! Come here this minute!

There is a pause, as Max summons up all the courage he has in him. He speaks slowly and clearly

Max No, ma'am!
Deanna Max ——
Max I've waited for a very long time to say that. In fact, it felt so good I'm gonna say it again. No, ma'am!

Everyone, except Deanna, applauds Max. He grins proudly

Joey Dirk, take her away!
Deanna No, not jail! Think what the papers will say! My reputation! My career!
Joey Well, there is one alternative.
Deanna Anything! I'll do anything!

Joey removes his apron and holds it out to Deanna

Deanna A waitress? Me?? I couldn't!
Joey Jail it is, then. Dirk? Take her away.
Deanna No, wait! Oh, all right, all right! (*She puts on the apron, with disgust*)

Joey And your first job is to make shakes for everyone — on the house!

Lighting change to rock and roll style: bright colours and flashing lights

Everyone cheers

*If the chorus has been split into groups for the show, the full company should
enter to take part in the final number and curtain calls*

No. 12 Shake, Ripple & Roll (Reprise)

All	Shake, Ripple and Roll!
	Shake, Ripple and Roll!
	We wanna —
	Shake, Ripple and Roll!
	Yeah baby!
	Shake, Ripple and Roll!
	There ain't nothin' to it
	All the kids'll wanna do it
	Have a Shake, Ripple and Roll!

Joey
Cohen ⎫
Dirk ⎬ If you're in the candy mood
Chuck ⎭ You can be the coolest dude with a shake

All   Shake shake
               Shake shake

Waitresses (*except Deanna*) If you really got the lick
               You can be the hippest chick with a shake

All   Shake shake
               Shake shake

Deanna ⎫ So don't walk on by
Max   ⎬ Won't ya come on in and try a little shake

All   Shake, Ripple and Roll!
               Shake, Ripple and Roll!
               We wanna...
               Shake, Ripple and Roll!
               Yeah baby!
               Shake, Ripple and Roll!

There ain't nothin' to it
All the kids'll wanna do it
Have a Shake, Ripple and Roll!

There ain't nothin' to it
All the kids'll wanna do it
Have a Shake
(*Speaking*) Shake Shake!
(*Singing*) Ripple and Roll!

The Lighting cross-fades to general bright full-stage wash for bows

No. 12a Bows

No. 12b Encore (Reprise: Another Day)

All (*singing*)   It's just another day, hanging round the store,
Another day, no different than before.
The sodas flow with Uncle Angelo
Uh-o uh-o
Poodle skirts, ponytails a-swishin'.
All the guys for Thunderbirds are wishin'.
Don't drive slow to Uncle Angelo
Uh-o uh-o
Summer's hot, we gotta keep the temp'rature low.
Uncle Angelo's is the place to go!
Uh-o
A-whoa whoa whoa whoa
Rockin' and a-rollin' in our saddle shoes
The neatest way to beat the summer blues.
We go, go, go to Uncle Angelo
Uh-o uh-o
We go, go, go to Uncle Angelo!
Uncle Angelo!

No. 12c Exit Music

THE END

FURNITURE & PROPERTY LIST

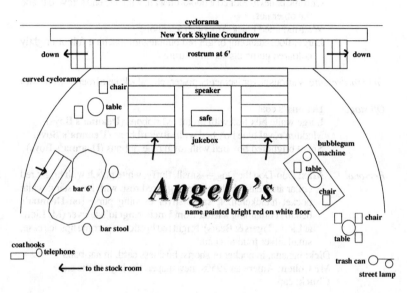

cyclorama

New York Skyline Groundrow

down ← rostrum at 6' down

curved cyclorama

chair

table

speaker

safe

jukebox

bubblegum machine

table

Angelo's

name painted bright red on white floor

chair

bar 6'

bar stool

chair

table

coat hooks

telephone

← to the stock room

trash can

street lamp

On stage: Interior of a 1950s' ice-cream parlour

Rostra

Chrome/bright red jukebox. Not practical, but with a speaker set behind it. *In it*: safe with combination lock. *In safe*: Uncle Angelo's will

Bar with bright red sides, royal blue top and chrome edging. *Behind bar on shelf*: royal blue/bright red sundae glasses filled with expanding foam and straws; ice-cream cone filled with expanding foam; empty sundae glasses; pile of white tea-towels; chrome dustpan and brush; bright red, white and royal blue large feather duster; chrome broom; a white half-apron; American 1950s' newspaper with eye-hole cut out. *On bar*: 4 round chrome trays, each with one small bright red notepad, short bright red pencil attached to each pad with silver ribbon for the **Waitresses**; American 1950s' cash register; chrome straw holder and red/white/blue straws; chrome serviette holder with bright red/royal blue paper serviettes; two chrome sugar shakers. *Front of bar*: 4 chrome bar stools

Three round chrome tables (1 set on rostra). *On each table*: chrome
serviette holder and bright red/royal blue paper serviettes; silver
card menu with bright red "Uncle Angelo's" on front (optional
dressing).

Two chrome chairs at table on rostra

Three chrome chairs around each of the other tables

Chrome panel of four coat hooks on wall, with one end screwed in and
the other not

Wall-mounted black American telephone

Large, floor-standing bright red bubblegum machine full of brightly
coloured gumballs set on rostrum

General dressing: Various advertisements, posters etc. Blackboard menu on one wall

Off stage: **Deanna**'s coat

Large white box tied with bright red ribbons (**Deanna's Boys**)

Medium royal blue box tied with silver ribbons (**Deanna's Boys**)

Small bright red box tied with royal blue ribbons (**Deanna's Boys**)

Personal: **Max**: Doo-Doo the Dog — small, fluffy, white pooch with bright red
collar and leash; buttonhole bright red rose with long stem; white
pocket handkerchief; small silver evening purse (on **Deanna**'s
behalf) containing a letter from **Uncle Angelo**'s lawyer (Mr Lions
at Lions, Tigers & Bears); bright red lipstick in chrome lipstick case;
small silver fountain pen.

Dirk: banana, in pocket of shorts; business card, in hat-band

Mr Cohen: American 1950s' newspaper; the keys to the store

Chuck: cap

COSTUME PLOT

Dirk Manley
Bright yellow T-shirt with pocket
Bright green baggy shorts
Bright orange ankle socks
Bright red baseball boots
Full length tan raincoat with belt and collar
Tan felt fedora with hat-band

Joey Nobody
Bright red T-shirt with white "Angelo's" logo
Bright red cotton trousers with turn-ups
White ankle socks
Bright red baseball boots
White half-apron (set onstage)
Bright red and white striped short fast food paper hat
Large cartoon picture of ice-cream cone painted on upper right arm (face paints)

Mr Cohen
Bright red long-sleeved shirt (sleeves rolled up)
Royal blue tie
Bright red cotton trousers with turn-ups
White ankle socks
Bright red baseball boots
Bright red and white striped short fast food paper hat

Cherry, Peaches, Pumpkin, Honey
Bright red T-shirt with white "Angelo's" logo
Bright red circular mini-skirt
White half apron with rounded corners and face trim
White ankle socks
White jazz shoes

Chuck
Dark blue jeans
Tight-fitting round-necked white T-shirt with bright red 5-point star logo on front
White ankle socks
Bright red baseball boots
Bright red baseball cap (no logo)

Deanna la Domme
Bright red velvet figure-hugging full length evening gown with *diamanté* and
   blue crystal trim, with a split up one side of the skirt
Black feather boa
One bright red and one royal blue feather in hair
Black tights
Black character shoes with Cuban heel
Diamanté necklace, earrings etc

Max the Chauffeur
Black dinner suit
White shirt
Bright red bow tie
Black ankle socks
Black jazz shoes
Black chauffeur's cap with bright red hat-band

Deanna's boys
Black dinner suit
White shirt
Bright red bow tie
Black ankle socks
Black jazz shoes

Male Chorus
Dark blue jeans
Tight-fitting round-necked white T-shirt with red 5-point star logo on front
White ankle socks
Bright red or royal blue baseball boots

*Female Chorus
Calf-length circular bright red skirts with bright red net petticoats
Tight-fitting round-necked white T-shirt with red 5-point star logo on front
Royal blue neckerchief
Royal blue ankle socks
White jazz shoes
Bright red, white or royal blue hair accessories

*Female Chorus
Calf-length circular royal blue skirts with royal blue net petticoats
Tight-fitting round-necked white T-shirt with red 5-point star logo on front
Bright red neckerchief
Bright red ankle socks
White jazz shoes
Bright red, white or royal blue hair accessories

*Half the female chorus in one colour combination, the other half in the other
combination.

LIGHTING PLOT

Property fittings required: Optional street lamp for **Dirk Manley** as Narrator

To open: House lights at full and open stage preset

Cue 1	Front of House clearance *House lights and preset out* *Special on* **Dirk Manley**	(Page 1)
Cue 2	**Dirk Manley**: "I wanna tell you a little story." *The Lights slowly change up to general morning* *full-stage wash*	(Page 1)
Cue 3	**Chuck**: "But we just *love* your flavours!" *Cross-fade to general blue full-stage wash* *Spot on* **Chuck**	(Page 8)
Cue 4	**Chuck**: "…I could dream…" *Begin rock & roll style lighting,* *bright colours and flashing lights*	(Page 8)
Cue 5	At the end of **No.2 Shake, Ripple & Roll** *Cross-fade to general bright full-stage wash*	(Page 10)
Cue 6	**Honey**: "— he doesn't even have us any more." *Cross-fade to general blue full-stage wash* *Plus individual shafts of white "heavenly" light* *Spot on* **Mr Cohen**	(Page 11)
Cue 7	At the end of **No.3 Angelo's an Angel Now** *Cross-fade to general bright full-stage wash*	(Page 13)
Cue 8	**Mr Cohen**: "We can't do anything until tomorrow." *Cross-fade to dim blue general wash* *Special on* **Dirk Manley**	(Page 13)
Cue 9	**Dirk Manley**: "The next day, things got even worse." *Cross-fade to general bright full-stage wash*	(Page 14)
Cue 10	**Mr Cohen**: "We're doomed." *Cross-fade to general bright orange and yellow wash* *Spot on* **Mr Cohen** *and* **Deanna**	(Page 17)

Cue 11   At the end of **No. 4 Where There's a Will**   (Page 18)
                Cross-fade to general bright full-stage wash

Cue 12   **Max**: "Oh yes, ma'am, absolutely."   (Page 19)
                Slow fade to night-time interior
                Special on **Dirk Manley**

Cue 13   **Dirk Manley**: "Mr Cohen came up with a good plan."   (Page 19)
                Fade special on **Dirk Manley**

Cue 14   **Waitresses**: "Chuck is *so* dreamy."   (Page 21)
                Slow fade to very dark blue general wash
                Small spot on **Joey**

Cue 15   At the end of **No.5 Nobody's Lament**   (Page 22)
                The lights slowly come up
                to general bright full-stage wash

Cue 16   **Dirk Manley**: "I am the King of Undercover!"   (Page 24)
                Begin rock & roll style lighting,
                bright colours and flashing lights
                Spot on **Dirk Manley**

Cue 17   At the end of **No.6 Undercover Blues**   (Page 25)
                Cross-fade to general bright full-stage wash

Cue 18   **Deanna**: "You look so… interesting."   (Page 27)
                Snap to general blue full-stage wash
                Spot on **Dirk Manley**

Cue 19   **Dirk**: "Meanwhile, Mr Cohen was frettin' about the will…" (Page 27)
                Snap restore general bright full-stage wash. Spot goes out

Cue 20   **Mr Cohen**: "When's it all gonna *end?*"   (Page 28)
                Snap to open-white footlights and general blue wash

Cue 21   At the end of **No.7 Somethin' Strange is Goin' On**   (Page 29)
                Snap to bright red, white and blue full-stage wash

Cue 22   At the end of **No.8 Today's the Day**   (Page 30)
                Cross-fade to general bright full-stage wash

Cue 23   **Deanna**: "Tell'em, boys."   (Page 32)
                Snap to red full-stage general wash
                Spot on **Deanna**

Cue 24	At the end of **No. 9 Deanna** *Cross-fade to general bright full-stage wash*	(Page 33)
Cue 25	**Joey** and **Mr Cohen**: "Argh!!" *Snap to open-white footlights only*	(Page 34)
Cue 26	As **Joey** places the coat on the coat hook *Snap to spot on jukebox* *General full-stage blue wash*	(Page 34)
Cue 27	As **Joey** and **Deanna** collide and fall over *Snap to general bright full-stage wash*	(Page 35)
Cue 28	**Waitresses**: " — Uncle Angelo's son!" *Snap to general dark blue wash* *Spot on* **Joey**	(Page 37)
Cue 29	At the end of **No.11 Nobody's Lament (reprise)** *Snap to general bright full-stage wash*	(Page 37)
Cue 30	**Joey**: "— on the house!" *Begin rock & roll style lighting* *Bright colours and flashing lights*	(Page 39)
Cue 31	At the end of **No. 12 Shake, Ripple & Roll (reprise)** *Cross-fade to general bright full-stage wash for bows*	(Page 40)

EFFECTS PLOT

*Optional sound effects cues

*Cue 1	At the end of **No.1 Another Day** *American street sounds, cars and footsteps, etc.* *brought in at low background level.*	(Page 5)
Cue 2	A customer puts a coin in the jukebox **No. 1a Will He Find Me?** (*on cassette provided*) *begins to play on the jukebox.* **American street sounds fade out*	(Page 6)
Cue 3	**Waitresses:** "We like this song!" **No. 1a Will He Find Me?** *gets a little louder*	(Page 6)
Cue 4	**Waitresses:** "When will he find me." **No. 1a** *fades down to background level* *until end of song*	(Page 7)
Cue 5	**Chuck:** "... 'Nobody's Ice-Cream Parlour!'" **No. 1a** *is faded out slowly if it hasn't finished yet*	(Page 7)
*Cue 6	At the end of **No.2 Shake, Ripple & Roll** *American street sound is crept back* *in at low background level*	(Page 10)
Cue 7	**Dirk Manley:** "Until the phone rang…" *The telephone rings* (*on cassette provided*) *until* **Mr Cohen** *answers it*	(Page 10)
*Cue 8	**Joey:** " It means closest relative." *American street sound is faded out*	(Page 11)
*Cue 9	At the end of **No.3 Angelo's an Angel Now** *American street sounds are* *crept back in at low background level*	(Page 13)
*Cue 10	**Mr Cohen:** "We can't do anything until tomorrow." *The American street sounds are faded out*	(Page 13)
*Cue 11	**Dirk Manley:** "Why am I asking you? " *The American street sounds are crept back in*	(Page 14)

*Cue 12   **Dirk Manley**: "... walked through the door ..."   (Page 14)
           American street sounds
           become a little louder

*Cue 13   As soon as **Deanna** has entered   (Page 14)
           American street sounds fade
           quickly to low background level

*Cue 14   **Mr Cohen**: "Wow, I'm a genius."   (Page 17)
           The American street sound is faded out

*Cue 15   At the end of **No. 4 Where There's a Will**   (Page 18)
           The American street sound is
           crept back in at low background level

*Cue 16   **Max**: "Oh yes, ma'am, absolutely."   (Page 19)
           The American street sound is faded out

*Cue 17   At the end of **No. 5 Nobody's Lament**   (Page 22)
           The American street sound is
           crept back in at low background level

*Cue 18   **Dirk Manley**: "It's all part of my plan."   (Page 24)
           The American street sound is faded out

*Cue 19   At the end of **No.6** Undercover Blues   (Page 25)
           The American street sound is
           crept back in at low background level

*Cue 20   **Deanna**: "You look so…interesting."   (Page 27)
           The American street sound is faded out

Cue 21   A customer puts a coin in the jukebox   (Page 27)
           FX: Will He Find Me? *begins to play on the jukebox*
           (*needle stuck version on cassette provided*)

Cue 22   **Mr Cohen** kicks the jukebox   (Page 28)
           FX: Will He Find Me? *snaps out*

*Cue 23   At the end of **No. 8 Today's the Day**   (Page 30)
           The American street sound
           is crept back in at low background level

*Cue 24   **Deanna**: "And you're all fired."   (Page 32)
           The American street sound is faded out

Cue 25   As **Joey** hangs the coat on the coat hook   (Page 34)
           A secret panel opens in the jukebox
           to reveal a safe door with a combination lock

MADE AND PRINTED IN GREAT BRITAIN BY
LATIMER TREND & COMPANY LTD PLYMOUTH
MADE IN ENGLAND